OLYSLAGER AUTO LIBRARY

Wreckers and Recovery Vehicles

compiled by the OLYSLAGER ORGANISATION

research by Denis N. Miller

edited by Bart H. Vanderveen

FREDERICK WARNE
London and New York

THE OLYSLAGER AUTO LIBRARY

This book is one of a growing range of titles on major transport subjects.
Titles published so far include:

Copyright © Olyslager Organisation NV 1972

First published 1972 by Frederick Warne (Publishers) Ltd, London

Revised edition 1979

Library of Congress Catalog Card Number 77-186750

ISBN 0 7232 1466 2

Photoset and printed in Great Britain by BAS Printers Ltd, Over Wallop, Hampshire D5995.779

INTRODUCTION

The introduction of the Model T Ford, or 'Tin Lizzie' as it was more affectionately known, brought motoring to the masses. Many who had never even dreamed of driving a car now found themselves proud owners of the ubiquitous 'T', the world's first mass-produced motor vehicle.

With the pleasures of motoring came the trials and tribulations of routine servicing and maintenance, plus the ever present threat of accident repairs. Such was the enthusiasm of the early motorist, however, that he often dealt with these tasks himself. On the other hand, there were others who had no wish to sully their hands with such mundane tasks. Thus, newly established garages and service stations were quick to realize the potential in this field.

At first, ordinary private cars were used to tow stricken vehicles back to the repair shops, but as the motor vehicle became heavier, more sophisticated and capable of crashing at higher speeds, so the need for more specialized recovery equipment became apparent. The light pick-up, carrying a length of tow rope or chain, was the next step, as this could be used as a general runabout for the collection and delivery of spares when not required for breakdown work. Soon this was equipped with a light hoist mounted at the rear and since then competitors in the vehicle recovery field have striven to 'out-do' each other in maximum lift capacities, recovery capabilities and speed of operation, so that the recovery vehicle has now become an extremely specialized vehicle type, tailored to the individual whims and requirements of each operator.

Broadly speaking, there are three basic types of recovery vehicle. These are the wrecker, the breakdown tender and the recovery vehicle itself. For our purposes, a wrecker is the twin-boom type so popular in the United States, the breakdown tender is one which carries a host of additional breakdown tackle (such as blocks, chains, jacks, oxy-acetylene cutting equipment, etc.) and generally features a box-type body with rear hoist equipment, and the recovery vehicle covers all other known types, including breakdown trucks, winch tractors and the like.

The first extensive use of medium-weight breakdown vehicles was during World War I when considerable quantities of otherwise standard cargo trucks were fitted with a rear hoist mechanism and used in all fields of war. When these were disposed of after the war, many were acquired by civilian transport contractors who, until then, had used their own general haulage vehicles as towing trucks in an emergency. Now, operators as well as garages and repair shops, were running their own recovery equipment.

World War II had an even greater effect upon the recovery business. Since 1945 vast quantities of ex-Services vehicles have been auctioned off to civilian operators. Many have been sold as complete recovery outfits, the majority with all-wheel drive, whilst others have been converted for or by the operator solely for recovery work. Today, a large percentage of recovery machinery is of ex-Services stock.

Now, however, there is a trend towards brand-new vehicles and equipment. The days of assembling one's own recovery crane from odds and ends lying around one's premises have largely disappeared. Specialist firms have sprung up, supplying and often fitting the complete power recovery equipment to a chassis of one's choice.

Recovery crew training is another aspect largely ignored in the past. This too, is becoming a 'must' for the operator with an eye for business. Without an efficient recovery service he is doomed to failure.

A subject such as this is, of course, extremely complex and therefore very difficult to break down into suitable sub-sections. In the first instance we have described the basic types, methods of recovery and principal equipment manufacturers, and then dealt with the numerous chassis types and chassis/equipment combinations.

3A : 1914. The first Ernest Holmes twin-boom wrecker was mounted on a 1914 Cadillac, now beautifully restored.
3B : 1937. This 3-ton Bedford WTH was typical of pre-World War II recovery outfits operating in the United Kingdom. Spurlings designed, equipped and operated the vehicle.
3C : 1972. Ford's main dealers, Hartford Motors of Oxford, acquired this Ford D1000 outfit, featuring an 8-ton TFL T.8 hydraulic crane.

3A

3B

3C

SELECTING A WRECKER

To the general public a recovery vehicle is merely a truck fitted with lifting equipment for recovering broken-down or wrecked road vehicles. To the operator it is a specialist piece of machinery worth its weight in gold, it must be capable of tackling any task placed before it and, above all, it must be reliable and efficient under all conditions.

In selecting a wrecker one must first consider all requirements. Obviously, a heavy recovery outfit is of more use to an operator within striking distance of a main trunk route or motorway intersection than to one sited in a small town fifteen miles or more from the nearest main route. Frequency of use, travelling distances, local traffic conditions and legal restrictions (where applicable) must all be considered. Speed of recovery and the average size and weight of vehicles to be recovered must also be borne in mind.

For light recovery work, mainly in heavy city traffic, a compact light tow truck is a major asset. For motorway or clearway work speed of operation takes priority, further advantages being manoeuvrability and the ability to reach the scene along the 'hard shoulder'.

In certain areas, where size restrictions are virtually non-existent, a heavy recovery outfit is seldom a handicap, particularly when one bears in mind the multiplicity of tasks it may be called upon to handle. Even so, it is not necessarily the size of a vehicle which dictates its recovery power. Indeed, the modern twin-boom wrecker is claimed to be one of the most versatile recovery units ever conceived and in certain areas of the United States police departments stipulate that a twin-boom machine must be sent for at all times as this is more capable of handling any eventuality.

The smallest outfits currently available are rigidly-mounted manual types for capacities of up to 1½ tons. These, of course, are used extensively on car recovery.

The smallest power wreckers generally fall into the 4 tons or under class, often featuring battery-powered winch gear and generally with single-boom equipment. Between 4 and 8 tons capacity, recovery cranes are generally driven by the engine power take-off but although this results in added winching ability the lifting power is still limited by boom and cable strength.

The 8/10 tons class is where twin-boom equipment now excels. Such a system comes into its own where space is restricted or where an extra heavy lift (more than the rig can normally handle) is necessary. Merely by anchoring the second boom, and possibly securing the rig further to nearby trees, etc., such a task is easily accomplished.

For still heavier tasks the 15/25 tons range is all-important. In the United States, twin-boom designs also predominate in this class but in many other countries (e.g. the United Kingdom) the single-boom design is favoured.

Above this are the 40- and 50-ton rigs, capable of recovering almost anything on wheels. These machines must be kept fully occupied to be economical. Only those operators specializing in heavy recovery could ever afford to run such giants.

4

It is often said that if one mounts an electric hoist on a standard ½-ton pick-up one has an ideal unit for light vehicle recovery. Generally, however, this is not the case. By the time the equipment, ballast and necessary tools have been added, there is little room for any additional payload and if the aforementioned articles are not carried then the vehicle can hardly operate as an efficient breakdown and recovery outfit. If one is intending to use one of these lighter models then certainly the rear suspension will require modification and if the original pick-up body is to be retained the hoist will have to be mounted over and to the rear of the back axle. Extra ballast will then be required to counteract a tendency to lift the front axle when winching.

The lightest truck which, with the minimum of modification, can successfully undertake such duties is the ¾/1-ton type. An important factor to bear in mind is that most ¾/1-tonners use truck parts whereas the ½-tonner is normally based on a private car chassis. Thus, for reliability alone, the heavier model is more ably suited.

The 15/25 tons class also requires special consideration. It is considered that a chassis of between 20,000 and 28,000 lb GVW should be specified. If possible, this should be specially strengthened at manufacturing stage rather than by adding flitch plates (extra strips of steel welded to the chassis frame sidemembers) to a secondhand model. An ex-Services vehicle in this category usually requires no essential modification, however. For these heavier applications, a heavy-duty front axle (preferably driven) is also an advantage in that it will provide additional weight where it is really necessary.

Ancillary recovery equipment is always extremely important. The operator must be prepared for every conceivable eventuality, and many inconceivable ones. For non-towable wrecks, and for automatic transmission vehicles where the propeller shaft cannot be disconnected, special wheeled 'dollies' (or 'towing ambulances') are carried and some recovery rigs even haul close-coupled 4-wheeled drawbar trailers for this purpose.

After considering these points, and many more, the recovery specialist is ready to choose the equipment best suited to him but with an untrained crew he is wasting his money. But how does one actually recover a vehicle?

5C

5A

5B

4: A ¾-ton Commer 'Superpoise' pick-up was ideal for light city recovery work. Messrs Brew Brothers Ltd., of London, used this 1960 version minus tailgate and equipped with a light tubular strut jib with manual winch at the forward end of the all-steel body. Even at these low weights rear stabilizers are desirable.

5A: The Weld/Built Body Co.'s 6 tons capacity Model 3B-20 is typical of the American light battery-operated class. This Chevrolet '30' of the City of New York Police Department features Weld/Built's Model 102A body of austere but robust design. Hoist levers are located on each side of the body behind the rear axle. Thus, the operator has all movements under his immediate control.

5B: For 10-ton lifts the Holmes '500' twin-boom power Wrecker is gaining fast in popularity, both in the United States and abroad. This example was mounted on a left-hand drive GMC chassis/cab by Dial-Holmes (England) Ltd.

5C: Bedford's R-Series truck is a particularly popular all-wheel drive model used by recovery operators. The grocery and supermarket chain of J. Sainsbury Ltd. employs a vast fleet of Bedford trucks, including this R-Type with all-steel bodywork by Reynolds Boughton Ltd. The dropsides facilitate slewing of the manually-operated twin-lift crane.

No matter what the circumstances, the efficient recovery operator must be prepared for any eventuality. Whether it is a car in a ditch or an 'artic' on its side, his crew must be capable of dealing with it or, at the least, know where additional heavy lifting equipment capable of the recovery can be obtained with the minimum of delay.

The idea behind vehicle recovery is not to recover a vehicle as rapidly as possible (although this, of course, must be taken into account), but to recover that vehicle in such a way that further damage is minimal. What is possibly a badly damaged vehicle can become an insurance 'write-off' if handled by an inexperienced or badly-equipped crew. To avoid this, many insurance companies even stipulate which recovery services may be used.

7A

6 : MOTORWAY MADNESS! Such scenes of devastation can affect even the toughest of recovery crews. Three recovery rigs can be seen here. Two are ex-Services AEC 'Matador' 4 × 4 models and the third a Hertfordshire Fire Service R-Series Bedford with Holmes twin-boom equipment.

7A: Overturned commercial vehicles are a common occurrence. Here we have 6½ tons of jam, marmalade and mincemeat blocking the road. The recovery crew are attempting to pass a hawser (heavy gauge wire rope) right round the body and chassis of this Leyland 'Comet' in order to winch it back onto its wheels.

7B: This Atkinson 'artic' ran off the road, luckily with only very minor damage. The unique Unipower/Holmes 'Invader', a special 4 × 4 machine in the same weight class as the 4 × 4 'Matador', was brought in to winch it back to road level. Rear wheels of the 'Invader' were well chocked (using the kerb where possible) and cable from the left-hand winch drum attached to the rear bogie of the semi-trailer (To avoid damage this would normally be attached to the semi-trailer chassis. This design, however, was chassisless.)

7C: Whilst of rugged construction and with ample winching power, the ex-Services SV/2S Scammell, based on the 'Pioneer' 6 × 4 model, is often limited under certain conditions. In this instance, it had to be parked at right angles to the overturned van, a Morris 'FM' telephone engineer's vehicle, in order to winch it back onto its wheels. If, for example, a twin-boom design had been employed, the wrecker could have been parked alongside the van and removed from the road with the minimum of manoeuvring and with little disruption to traffic.

7B

7C

There are many other pitfalls awaiting breakdown gangs. Automatic transmission vehicles must be treated with extreme care as an ordinary rigid tow will badly damage the transmission unless the drive-line is disconnected and secured to the chassis frame, or, in the case of heavier vehicles, the half-shafts are removed. In the case of private cars with automatic transmission systems it is often best to use a special 'towing ambulance' inserted under the rear wheels, or even a full transporter trailer. Commercial vehicles with tiltcabs are yet another problem. It is advisable to suspend-tow these from the rear, having first locked the steering gear, as contact with the lifting equipment may result in cab distortion affecting tilt capabilities. Recovery crews are advised at all times to use rigid towbars when not employing the suspended-tow system and a specially designed spacer bar between the rear of the recovery rig and front of the towed vehicle when utilizing the suspended-tow method.

9B

9A

9C

8: The results of a 'jack-knife' accident involving an articulated lorry can be amongst the most difficult of all recoveries. This 32-ton GCW Atkinson/York outfit 'jack-knifed' on the M1 Motorway in 1970. The wreckers used on this occasion were ex-Services 6 × 6 models, one with Dial-Holmes twin-boom gear and the other with a specially fabricated fixed-jib design. Both had to be positioned on the motorway embankment and, between them, manoeuvre the artic's tractor portion clear of the semi-trailer landing legs. The vehicle is already a 'write-off' so further damage is relatively unimportant.

9A: An articulated lorry has careered into a river, leaving the tractor portion almost totally submerged. The combined efforts of a '980' Diamond T and a BMC 'Mastiff', both with Holmes twin-boom equipment, plus a Coles truck-crane of Dial-Holmes Plant Hire, were needed to haul the truck back to road level. While the 'T'

provided hauling power, the 'Mastiff' was on hand to guide the artic onto the road. The truck-crane lifted the front of the artic clear of the mud.

9B: Just one of the many fatal accidents a recovery crew can be faced with. A fully-laden 22-ton container crushed a Ford 'Cortina' estate car after the artic upon which the container was travelling overturned. In this view, preparations are being made for the Hertfordshire Fire Service's twin-boom wrecker (see also Fig. 6) to raise one corner of the container so that the 'Cortina' can be hauled clear.

9C: Two recovery rigs—a Harvey Frost-equipped Leyland 'Tiger' (formerly a passenger vehicle) and an ex-Services Austin K6 6 × 4 breakdown gantry vehicle—attempt to right a Leyland double-decker bus. With such a wide carriageway this should prove relatively simple but all too frequently the road is less than half this width.

10A : A 10-ton articulated Bedford has collided with a wall and broken its back. How does one recover such a vehicle ?
10B : An attempt is made to haul the Bedford away from the wall, utilizing the winch gear of a 4 × 4 R-Series Bedford.
10C : The semi-trailer is undamaged so the next step is to uncouple this from the wrecked tractor. Because the coupling is jammed, the recovery vehicle is withdrawn to the rear of the semi-trailer and chains attached to the chassis frame. Chocks are placed behind the wrecked tractor's wheels to prevent unwanted movement of the tractor unit.
10D : By using a crowbar on the automatic coupling, tractor and semi-trailer portions are separated although the landing wheels do not drop 'true'.

Independent and air suspension systems are yet another problem; care must be taken to ensure that the wheels or axles do not drop out completely during recovery. The most important 'golden rule', however, is never to attach winch cable or lifting tackle to anything but specially provided towing eyes or vehicle chassis frames. Allied to this is the fact that, with heavy vehicles in particular, winch power must never be applied to axles or to one corner of the chassis frame. The former may result in the ripping out of an axle and the latter in severe frame distortion. Furthermore, when righting an overturned vehicle, cable must be paid out right round the vehicle and timber or similar packing inserted between cable and bodywork both to prevent body damage and to spread the load force.

The following situations will provide some insight into the many varied tasks a recovery crew can be called upon to undertake and the methods employed to surmount such problems. It must be remembered that no two jobs are the same. Similar methods may be employed but every task should be regarded as totally different.

10A

10C

10B

10D

WRECK RECOVERY

11A : The recovery crane, a specially fabricated hydraulic unit with a fixed hook and chain lifting system has raised the front of the Bedford clear of the ground so that this can be hauled away and a replacement tractor coupled to the semi-trailer.

11B : The new unit is first used to straighten the semi-trailer landing wheels. Using the method shown is *not* advisable as it could result in buckling of the tractor's chassis frame.

11C : Even with the high ground clearance of a 4 x 4 recovery vehicle, there is little space for lifting the front of the 'TK' clear of the road surface.

11D : Damage to the Bedford is clear. The frame is broken just ahead of the rear axle. The lift chains have been attached both to the forward ends of the chassis and to the front bumper. A further chain connects the rear of the recovery rig to the tractor's front axle, reducing 'to-and-fro' movement during towing.

11A

11C

11B

11D

BENDIX WESTINGHOUSE LTD.

In 1964 Westinghouse Brake & Signal Co. Ltd. in Britain took over Mann Egerton's Engineering Division, continuing production of Mann Egerton-designed recovery equipment under the Westinghouse brand name.

The Company was later renamed Bendix Westinghouse Ltd., manufacturing as standard former Mann Egerton manually-operated recovery cranes of up to 7½ tons capacity. This type of equipment has now been discontinued.

Only one very heavy machine was built, this being supplied for test purposes to the Indian Government. The heavy-duty 10-ton slewing cranes manufactured by Mann Egerton up to the time of takeover are now produced by Messrs Reynolds Boughton Ltd.

12 : Heaviest of the Westinghouse range was the 7½-ton twin-lift model. This was manually-controlled, each hook having an individual capacity of 3½ tons. Winding handles were provided on both sides of the crane base, one for each hook, and in this instance body-work was by Bonallack & Sons Ltd. on a 7-ton Austin FF K140 chassis.

13A : Mann Egerton's 5-ton twin-lift model first appeared some fifteen years ago. This, the Westinghouse version, was identical but featured a Type 'H' Westinghouse 'towing ambulance', designed for one ton lifts. This was stored vertically at the rear of the vehicle when not in use. Once again the traditional stylish body was a feature.

13B : The 7½-ton rig has also been mounted on vehicles in the 10 tons capacity class. An AEC 'Matador' 4 × 4 outfit, beautifully bodied by Eastern Coachworks Ltd., exemplified this. The main cab structure incorporated many components common to ECW-bodied passenger models, of which much of the Eastern Counties fleet was composed. Thus, the ability to interchange parts was an added attraction.

13A

13B

EKA (BÄRGNINGSBILAR EKA AB)

15A

Although expensive, EKA recovery equipment is rapidly gaining popularity in its native Scandinavia, where operating conditions during the greater part of the year dictate a sophisticated but easily actuated power recovery system.

Messrs Bärgningsbilar EKA AB, of Gårdstigen, Sweden, designers and manufacturers of this equipment, offer a range of 3/4-, 10/15- and 20/40- ton models, all utilizing hydraulic or electro-hydraulic power.

The EKA system is a complete departure from established methods of vehicle recovery. Not only is the lifting force applied from beneath the stricken vehicle instead of from above but, as an option, all operations can be radio-controlled, enabling one operator to cope with large recovery problems almost single-handed.

All models feature a single lifting arm, elevated by a hydraulic ram located at the rear of the machine. This arm can be fitted with various attachments to combat most problems but of these a special rack for sliding beneath the wheels of a disabled vehicle is most common for the lighter tasks, with lifting forks popular for heavier work. Electric or hydraulic winches can be specified and the winch cable can be run off the head of the boom when lifting from overhead becomes necessary.

15B

15C

14: EKA bodywork is especially well designed, incorporating ample tool and equipment lockers. This Volvo N86 is equipped for light vehicle recovery, using the special lifting rack into which the front or rear wheels of the car are driven and secured by clamps, thereby minimizing the possibility of further damage in transit.

15A: The F86 Volvo was a popular choice of EKA operators. Not only can the single hydraulic ram be seen in this view but also the hydraulic boom extension controls (through opened hatch in rear body side).

These controls can also be radio-controlled.

15B: An EKA Type D 20-ton recovery outfit on Volvo FB88 6 × 4 chassis was evaluated by the British Army in 1970. Prior to this, it was a demonstrator in the livery of Volvo and EKA UK concessionaires Ailsa Trucks Ltd.

15C: By 1978 the British Army had several Leyland/Scammell Crusader 6 × 4 trucks with EKA D2030B equipment (single lift boom with lift and tow capacity of 7500 kg) for recovery of logistic vehicles.

GAR WOOD INDUSTRIES INC.

Thirty-one years old Garfield A. Wood produced his first machine, a special hydraulic hoist, in 1912 and was quick to take advantage of the demand for this type of equipment. In 1922 his Company became known as Gar Wood Industries Inc. and henceforward Gar Wood products included all manner of items of welded steel construction, such as dump bodies, earthmoving equipment, mechanical handling appliances, refuse collectors, etc.

16C

16A   16B

During World War II practically all production was diverted to Government contracts, amongst which was a high proportion of wrecking and vehicle and aircraft recovery equipment. Single- and twin-boom designs were produced, of which the former included the unusual six-wheel drive single slewing boom types with fifth wheel couplings designed primarily for the US Army Air Force and intended for operation with semi-trailers conveying wrecked aircraft.

16D

16A: Single-boom slewing wreckers of the US Army Air Force were based mainly on Biederman, Federal and Reo 6 × 6 chassis, with a few on Autocar 4 × 2 and 4 × 4 models. With stabilizers in the lift position, this rear view of a Federal C-2 Model 605 shows the underslung rear winch, fifth wheel coupling and 10 tons capacity Gar Wood gooseneck boom.

16B: The M1 heavy wrecker chassis was first produced by Ward LaFrance in 1940 as a 4-ton 6 × 6, equipped with a slewing type boom supplied by various wartime producers. This example of Gar Wood production featured power winches at front and rear and a heavy rear land anchor, the latter being a British Army modification.

16C: A much modified version of the Gar Wood-equipped M1 Ward LaFrance was operated by heavy hauliers Robert Wynn & Sons Ltd. The front end was rebuilt to accommodate a larger engine and an attractively styled body was added.

16D: Successor to the M1 series was the M1A1, manufactured by Kenworth and Ward LaFrance to a standardized specification. After the war Scottorn Ltd., of New Malden, Surrey, re-conditioned considerable numbers of former Services vehicles, notably for export. This was a typical example. The M1A1 was first introduced in 1943, incorporating a 5 tons capacity slewing crane and twin power winches by Gar Wood.

GAR WOOD INDUSTRIES INC.

17A: The Diamond T Model 969 was supplied to the armed forces as a double-boom 6 × 6 wrecking outfit. The Gar Wood equipment seen here was transferred from another Services wrecker, whilst the original Holmes body was retained.

17B: Mack Truck's LM-SW recovery outfit was supplied in two forms—as a single fixed boom or as a double-boom—both built by Gar Wood. The double-boom version was supplied to the Canadian Army with a lift capacity of 16 tons. The single-boom type was used by the British Army (see Fig. 45A).

17C: In Canada, Chevrolet C60S and C60L 4 × 4 chassis were both equipped by Gar Wood as double-boom outfits. The C60S was a short-wheelbase model of which this example was used in original form by Poplar Garage, Billingshurst, Sussex. Some versions had Holmes equipment.

17A

17B

17C

HARVEY FROST & CO. LTD.

18A

HF "DUAL" SALVAGE CRANE
For Breakdown and Loading (Ernest Lakes' Patent Applied for)
BRITISH MADE

HF DUAL CRANE

The most profitable investment in breakdown equipment.

18B

18C

18D

18A-B : Among the recovery equipment offered by Harvey Frost in 1929 was an unusual 'Dual' salvage crane, patented by Ernest Lake. This was basically similar to a sided lorry and when not used as a recovery machine could be used for general carrying work. When not required, the lifting equipment was stowed as shown in Fig. 18A but could be rapidly erected to lift from the rear (as in Fig. 18B), using twin hooks, for loads of up to 3 tons. Each hook had a capacity of 1½ tons.

18C : Early in the 1930's the Singer Company designed a special recovery outfit based on a light normal-control chassis of their manufacture. This was a 'Roadside Service & Salvage' vehicle which was duly recommended to all Singer agents. The design included a light Harvey Frost salvage crane and dropsides for use as work benches.

18D : Although this Canadian Chevrolet C15A with modified general service body was of 1941 vintage, the Harvey Frost crane was considerably older. This was known as the general duty type crane, designed for all light vehicle recovery tasks. The vertical winding wheel raised or lowered the lattice jib and a manually-operated chain hoist lifting system was employed.

Like so many motor industry pioneers, H. Harvey Frost began his business life selling bicycles and even building a design of his own—known as the Wellington. In 1903 he entered the garage equipment market with a small vulcanizer for repairing car tyres and tubes but, with tyre price reductions after World War I, demand for this fell to such an extent that the Company launched a complete range of imported garage equipment—by Weaver of the USA.

Demand exceeded supply. Thus, Harvey Frost & Co. Ltd. announced their own designs in this field, including a number of light and medium vehicle recovery and salvage cranes. The depression nearly saw the end of Harvey Frost. The Company's salvation was an amalgamation with Messrs Ernest Lake & Co. Ltd., manufacturers of equipment on behalf of Harvey Frost for many years.

By 1970, recovery equipment ranged from light hoists for use with pick-up trucks to 5-, 6- and 8-ton fixed and slewing types for twin-lift operation. All cranes were manually-controlled and a considerable proportion of production was exported.

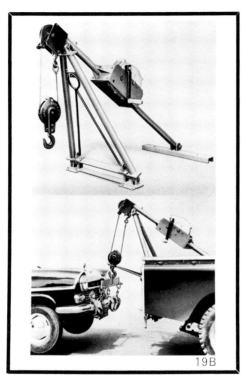

19B

19A: The forward-control Commer Q2, employed by the RAF during the last war, was once a popular choice in the recovery field. This pleasantly styled example, with sweeping body lines and easy access at the rear, carried a similar salvage crane to that shown in Fig. 18D.

19B: Lightest in Harvey Frost's 1970 range were the 'Towboy', a 2-wheeled hoist which could be hauled by a private car, and the 'HF Pick-up' crane, a detachable unit for use in conjunction with a Land-Rover, Austin 'Gipsy' or similar vehicle. Method of operation was simple and is clearly illustrated here.

19C: This 6-wheeled recovery rig was based on a 100-bhp Thornycroft 'Trusty' tandem-drive chassis with a 5-speed transmission. The slewing twin-lift crane was one of Harvey Frost's heavier types and the whole vehicle was designed and bodywork constructed by Messrs Martin Harper Ltd., of Guildford, Surrey.

19A

19C

THE ERNEST HOLMES CO.

Ernest Holmes was a pioneer in the vehicle recovery field. He ran an automobile repair business in Chattanooga, Tennessee, and, like so many others in this line of work, designed and built his own tow truck. This was not very satisfactory but in 1914 his first successful twin-(or double-)boom outfit appeared.

The advantages of the double-boom system were obvious from the start. Not only could such a rig recover vehicles from the side as well as from the rear, but by securing the cable from one boom to a suitable anchorage point the other boom could deal with weights equal to, and frequently heavier than, the rig itself.

By 1915 an improved and much simpler design had appeared and by the end of World War I the world's first power wrecker, again a twin-boom design, had entered service with the US Army. In 1920 the first two outfits sold to civilian operators left the Chattanooga works.

The 1930's saw a completely re-designed Holmes range, specially built to cope with the greater loads and increasingly complicated recovery operations which were by then becoming an everyday occurrence.

It was World War II, however, which brought about the real break-through in heavy-duty twin-boom designs, laying the foundations of the present Ernest Holmes organization. Sales are now rapidly increasing in many parts of the world (e.g. through Crane Fruehauf Service & Equipment Ltd in England and Interholmes Rescue AG, of Switzerland).

21C

20: The world's first power wrecker was a Holmes double-boom unit mounted on a USA (or 'Liberty') chassis. An interesting feature of the early Holmes twin-boom range was the positioning of the stabilizer legs within the main supports of the wrecker structure. Modern types feature special extensible legs, hinged at their upper ends.

21A: The first two twin-boom models for civilian customers, both manually-operated, were mounted on suitably modified car chassis. This Cadillac was one, featuring Model '485' lifting equipment on a lengthened 1912 chassis.

21B: The carriage of wrecks in this way was a common sight during the Twenties and Thirties. J. C. McLanahan's Model AA Ford sported Holmes '485' wrecking equipment.

21C: Dial-Holmes (England) Limited, one-time UK concessionaires for Holmes equipment, frequently adapted heavy haulage tractors for recovery work. This 6 × 6 Scammell 'Constructor' was previously owned by George Wimpey & Co. Ltd., civil engineers. the main modifications necessary being the replacement of the rear ballast box by the Holmes twin-boom equipment and body, and the addition of a heavily ballasted radiator brush guard and front bumper.

21A

21B

MANN EGERTON & CO. LTD.

Until 1964 Mann Egerton & Co. Ltd. was amongst the leaders in the recovery equipment market, much of production at that time going for export.

Gerard Mann, a young Cornishman, began business as an electrical engineer in Norwich in the nineteenth century, installing generating plants in country houses throughout East Anglia. He was quick to realize the potential of the motor vehicle and joined forces with Hubert Egerton, an engineer, to market private motor vehicles at the turn of the Century.

It was inevitable that a motor works, for servicing these vehicles and for building the individual body designs specified by Mann Egerton customers, would follow. Similarly, it was not long before the Company required some form of vehicle recovery system. One of the first took the form of a special trailer with winch and tilting platform, designed for the carriage of light motor vehicles. Early recovery apparatus was built at the Cromer Road works and carried on at these premises until this side of the business was disposed of in 1964.

In 1962 the Company added a 10 tons capacity slewing recovery crane to its extensive range. This was designed for use notably on heavy Scammell and AEC 6 × 6 chassis. In 1964, when the recovery equipment interests were sold, production of all light- and medium-duty types was passed to the Westinghouse Brake & Signal Co. Ltd. and the heaviest slewing models to Messrs Reynolds Boughton Ltd.

23A

23B

22 : How it used to be done. Soon after World War I Mann Egerton & Co. Ltd., added this RFC/RAF Crossley tender to its workshop assets (this was a former Royal Flying Corps vehicle, the RFC being renamed the Royal Air Force in 1918). The single-axle trailer, which was built in the Company's workshop, could be tilted as shown and a manual winch at the forward end used to load and unload light vehicles.

23A : Typical of manual types designed for modern light recovery work was this twin-lift 3-tonner which also had bodywork by Mann Egerton. The chassis was a petrol-engined FG-Series BMC.
23B : At the 1962 Commercial Motor Show the Company exhibited a new 10 tons capacity slewing wrecker known as the RC7 and mounted on a 17 ft 8 in wheelbase 6 × 6 Scammell 'Constructor' chassis. This was the largest breakdown vehicle in Mann Egerton's range, utilizing power hoisting and slewing but manual luffing and jib extension. It was supplied with a 5-ton 'towing ambulance' and numerous other items of equipment.

HERBERT MORRIS LTD.

With premises in Loughborough, Leicestershire, Messrs Herbert Morris Ltd. specialized in the manufacture of block and tackle and similar lifting equipment.

By the mid-1930's the London Fire Brigade was being called to so many non-fire emergencies every year that the then Chief Officer, Major C. C. B. Morris, MC, conceived a new type of appliance designed for light or heavy lifts, passing an order for this to Messrs Herbert Morris. The new equipment could be used for ordinary lifting tasks or for vehicle and crash recovery work, and it is interesting to note that this crane, mounted on a later Dennis chassis, was still in regular use with the Brigade as late as 1971.

Herbert Morris's general lifting tackle was often incorporated in the breakdown tender vehicle, employing the overhead gantry system (an example of this can be seen in Fig. 35A). Scammell Lorries Ltd. also used Morris lifting tackle in its 'Pioneer' and 'Explorer' recovery designs.

25A

24: The London Fire Brigade's first heavy breakdown vehicle (1935) with equipment by Herbert Morris was based on a short-wheelbase Dennis powered by a 6-cylinder 118-bhp engine. The chain-hoist crane, which was of the full slewing type, had a capacity of 8 tons and was manually-operated. Merely by altering the positions of a couple of gear wheels, the same winding handles could be used both for winching and jib elevation.

25A: In the mid-Fifties a similar crane, with a maximum capacity of 5 tons and equipped with a 2 tons capacity extension jib, was delivered to the Brigade. The earlier model was relegated to general towing work whilst the new addition joined the emergency fleet. This was also based on a Dennis chassis, incorporating additional breakdown equipment in the form of a 15-ton 'towing ambulance', a 6-ton 'ambulance', one 8- and one 10-ton hydraulic jack and a 24 tons capacity towbar. Other specialist emergency equipment was also carried.

25B: The original Herbert Morris crane was transferred to a new chassis during the early 1960's. Once again, the latest Dennis was employed, now with ample room for emergency equipment storage in an enclosed compartment behind the cab. Comparison with the original design shows increased locker space, more warning devices and a generally more functional appearance.

25B

REYNOLDS BOUGHTON LTD.

26A : Numerous examples of the Company's 3-ton swivel crane have been supplied for military use. This version, based on an R-Series Bedford, featured an extensible jib with power luffing and lifting. An 18,000 lb. capacity power winch, rear land anchor and various storage lockers were also specified. Bodywork was by Marshalls of Cambridge.

26B : A 5-ton version of this crane was also supplied on the Scammell 'Mountaineer' four-wheel drive chassis for desert use. A 'towing ambulance' was included in the specification.

26C : An early version of the Reynolds Boughton twin-boom design was mounted on a Mk 1 Ford Thames 'Trader' tipper chassis. This type of equipment was very similar to the Holmes design, although for many years Reynolds Boughton was the only Company manufacturing double-boom recovery systems in the UK, as Dial-Holmes imported the completed equipment from the USA.

26D : The majority of these double-boom types were mounted on the four-wheel drive R-Series Bedford. In this view, the outriggers, twin booms, 'towing ambulance' and rear winch rollers can be seen quite clearly.

Reynolds Boughton Ltd., established during the 1960's by the merger of W. J. Reynolds Ltd., of Dagenham, and T. T. Boughton & Sons Ltd., of Amersham, specializes in the supply of custom-built steel bodywork and equipment principally for military and overseas use. Amongst these have been recovery vehicle types of various designs.

The double-boom layout, similar to the Ernest Holmes system but with detail differences, has proved to be one of the most popular. The more conventional single-boom twin-lift layout frequently incorporated in Reynolds Boughton-equipped recovery rigs has often been the product of another recovery equipment manufacturer, such as Harvey Frost, and a 3 tons capacity single-boom single-life device, of which a number have been supplied to military authorities, was designed and constructed in association with Marshall of Cambridge (Engineering) Ltd.

26B 26C

26A

26D

REYNOLDS BOUGHTON LTD.

Heaviest machines in the range are 10 tons capacity extensible single-boom slewing designs normally fitted to AEC or Scammell 6 × 4 or 6 × 6 chassis. These were originally manufactured by Mann Egerton & Co. Ltd., using Boughton winches. Thus, when the light and medium recovery side of the Mann Egerton concern was taken over by the Westinghouse Brake and & Signal Co. Ltd., it was perhaps only natural that Reynolds Boughton should continue production of the heavier series.

27A

27A : In at least one instance an R-Series Bedford was converted by Reynolds Boughton to six-wheel drive with sand tyres for desert operation. The twin-boom wrecking equipment was positioned just ahead of the rear bogie and other features included double-insulated cab roof and a front-mounted power winch. Later models were based on M-Series Bedford chassis.

27B : Representative of the largest types manufactured by the Company, this Scammell 'Super Constructor' 6 × 6 was equipped with Reynolds Boughton 10 tons capacity slewing recovery crane, developed from earlier Mann Egerton designs. This was one of the last 'Super Constructor' models to be supplied, being fitted with a distinctive Motor Panels cab. Other equipment consisted of a vertical spindle Scammell winch, a heavy-duty 'towing ambulance' and a special rear land anchor.

27B

TFL (TRACEL FABRICATIONS LTD.)

In May 1966 Tracel Fabrications Ltd. (now TFL Cranes Ltd.) commenced manufacture of workshop cranes for use in garages, repair shops, etc. The Company's first venture into the heavy recovery equipment field was a 20 tons capacity hydraulic machine mounted on a Model 981 Diamond T for J. & H. Transport Ltd. This was in 1968, since when the recovery equipment range has been expanded to include lighter types as well. The heaviest and most popular model, however, was known as the T.20.

Primarily, the Company offers complete recovery vehicles rather than recovery cranes alone. Thus, a full range of services is offered, including the design and construction of bodywork, winches, lifting attachments, towbars, ballast bumpers, etc. The heaviest sector of the TFL system incorporates a fully-hydraulic calliper-type crane with powered boom extension and retraction, making this unique among British recovery outfits.

28 : TFL's first T.20 hydraulic recovery crane was mounted on a Model 981 Diamond T, with 500 ft Gar Wood winch and a cab taken from an ex-Services Morris-Commercial MRA1 4 × 4 model.

29A : The Company's T.2 salvage crane was designed for a safe working load of 2 tons and could be supplied with its own all-steel body as seen here. This particular machine was based on an ex-Services Austin K9 4 × 4 model featuring a power-driven winch.

29B : The Kenning Motor Group, of Chesterfield, Derbys., employs a fleet of these Guy 'Big J6' tandem-drive outfits on heavy recovery work. Each is powered by a Cummins NHK 220 diesel of 205-bhp capacity driving through an AEC 6-speed overdrive transmission. Each machine carries a TFL T.20 crane. The black and yellow diagonally-striped bumper bar is both for safety and recognition purposes.

29C : Even heavier was this 6 × 6 Scammell 'Constructor', formerly with Messrs Pickfords. This version, unlike that shown in Fig. 21C, remained in its original form, with the T.20 crane located neatly within the existing ballast box. Whilst the crane was capable of handling 20-ton loads, the winch could cope with a maximum pull of some 90 tons.

29A

29B

29C

WELD/BUILT BODY CO. INC.

30A

30B

The Weld/Built Body Co. Inc., of New York State, design and construct recovery equipment of up to 40 tons capacity. Like the Ernest Holmes Co., the Company's standard designs have all been of double-boom layout and are now especially popular with police departments, government authorities and the armed forces.

Weld/Built can also supply a range of specialist bodies and numerous recovery accessories. Some of the lighter ranges available were battery-powered; others were driven from a power take-off.

30A-B : Big sister to the New York Police Department's Chevrolet (Fig. 5A) was this International R200 with Weld/Built's Model 1C-10 15 tons capacity recovery gear. This model featured a 37,500 lb capacity power winch plus a self-locking manual worm winch for raising and lowering the boom. The body was a Model 101B Weld/Built design.
30C: Mid-1970s Chevrolet-based Weld/Built single-boom wrecker Model 3B40 with Model 102A body, carrying patented three-piece dolly. The telescopic boom extends 4 feet and lifts 4,000 pounds.

30C

WELD/BUILT BODY CO. INC.

31A

31B

31C

31A : Weld/Built's Model 6BHD with 104B body is a double-boom outfit of 20 tons capacity. This design includes twin power winches, one for each boom, each having a 22,500 lb pull and breaking point at 45,000 lb. Basis of this US Navy rig was an International 'Loadstar' 6 × 4 chassis.

31B : The 25 tons capacity 6C double-boom wrecking outfit is readily applied to a heavy-duty 4-wheeled chassis such as this Autocar.

A 101C body was used and a 20 tons capacity drag winch mounted on the rear deck.

31C : Largest in the Company's range is the 40-ton capacity Model 6CHD based, in this instance, on an impressive Autocar diesel chassis with twin front axles (8 × 4) and 'super single' tyres. A deviation from the standard variety of the 6CHD are the special telescopic booms (Model TB12).

WORLD WAR I BREAKDOWNS

The recovery vehicle as we know it was unheard of during the early years of World War I. This was the first major conflict involving motor transport on a large scale and it soon became clear that some form of recovery vehicle was necessary.

Early attempts in this direction were crude to say the least. Frequently, the recovery outfit consisted solely of a standard GS (general service) truck, equipped with a set of sheerlegs with block and tackle (for lifting stricken vehicles from trenches or craters) and odd lengths of chain, rope and timber. This type of vehicle was referred to as a 'first-aid' lorry.

Later, more specialized equipment appeared. These were also GS lorries, but were specially adapted for breakdown work. Fabricated jibs were fitted at the rear, employing cable from a manual winch at the forward end of the body. Sets of tools and a workbench were also carried and a most important item of equipment was a 'towing ambulance', often carried beneath the rear of the vehicle.

Of course, there were exceptions to these, such as the Holmes twin-boom power wrecker introduced at the very end of the war (Fig. 20A).

33A

33C

33B

32 : Typical of the earliest World War I 'first-aid' units was this Karrier (background). In this view a second Karrier is being lifted from a bomb crater using the breakdown vehicle's sheerlegs.

33A : The next development was the use of rear-mounted crane jibs using a block and tackle lifting system. This early Leyland was just one of the new breed.

33B : A staff car (formerly a taxicab) is being recovered from a ditch by a Peerless breakdown outfit. Crane equipment was now more ruggedly constructed and numerous tools, including picks, shovels, crowbars, etc., were carried along the body sides. The canvas tilt was easily run back to the forward end of the body to give those operating the winch a clearer view of the field of operations.

33C : A close-up of the rear of a similar vehicle, again on a chain-drive Peerless 3-ton chassis, reveals the special screw jacks or stabilizers, heavy-duty crane jib and the 2-wheeled 'towing ambulance' slung behind the rear axle.

34 : Of the twelve Associated Daimler 802 model 6-wheeled passenger vehicles supplied to the London General Omnibus Co. in 1927/8 (the first 6-wheeled buses on London streets), no fewer than four were converted into breakdown tenders in 1936/7. The elaborately-equipped bodies were by Eagle Engineering, of Warwick, and all four remained in service as breakdown tenders longer than they did as passenger models. Sold out of service in 1951, they had all disappeared by 1955.

35A

35A : A close-up of the rear of one of these interesting Associated Daimlers illustrates how the rear of the chassis was terminated behind the rear wheels and how a suspended tow was executed, using the Morris chain hoist system and a special stabilizer (or spacer) bar.

35B : A former East Surrey double-decker bus was also adapted for this purpose. Again the chain hoist and stabilizer bar were employed. Note the safety rails beneath the sides of the tender—a legacy from the days of passenger operation.

35C : In 1948 a batch of Leyland 'Titan' PD2/1 double-decker buses was supplied new to the City of Plymouth Transport Department. No. 319 (DJY 949) in this batch was converted as shown following withdrawal from passenger service in 1963. Although not as manoeuvrable as short-wheelbase models, the Leyland's long wheelbase in this case as the forward portion of the vehicle acted as a counterbalance when lifting. A 5/6-ton Harvey Frost twin-lift slewing crane was carried and the chassis frame shortened behind the rear axle.

BUS AND COACH CONVERSIONS

During the inter-war period passenger vehicle operators found their vehicles increasing both in size and weight, making recovery of such machines more and more difficult. Many operators would send out a small lorry for the majority of incidents and if a tow was required an existing passenger-carrying vehicle would be employed. Because of this, a suspended tow was virtually unheard of in this business.

One answer to the problem was to convert withdrawn passenger models into recovery outfits. The most common layout adopted was that of breakdown tender, using an overhead gantry system with rear chain hoist. This, of course, necessitated shortening the chassis at

35B

the rear and often converting the interior into a complete mobile workshop.

More recently there have been even one or two more drastic conversions involving the fitting of the standard design recovery crane at the rear. Generally, however, the modern passenger vehicle operator now prefers to run a heavy-duty recovery outfit, frequently based on an ex-Services chassis.

35C

PRIVATE CAR CONVERSIONS

Although, because of their generally low unladen weight, the conversion of private cars into light recovery outfits is not to be recommended, a few operators, particularly those with small country garages and repair shops, have found machines of this type most useful. Like the passenger vehicle operators described in preceding pages, this is one method of using vehicles at one's disposal to the maximum effect.

It is generally the larger and heavier cars, such as certain American models, which have been most popular in this field. Smaller types are also used however. In all cases, an uprated rear suspension should be regarded as essential. Without it, the vehicle would hardly be capable of recovering anything.

36A

36A: This French Ford 'Vedette' was originally supplied as a 4-door saloon. By welding the rear doors shut, and removing all coachwork above waist level and to the rear of the centre door pillars, it was converted into a pick-up with fabricated fixed crane bolted direct to the chassis frame sidemembers.

36B: Commercial version of the Ford 'Vedette' (Fig. 36A) was the 'Abeille', which had the same 2·2-litre side-valve V8 engine. This 'Abeille' (1954, Model F22C) was converted into a light recovery and towing vehicle simply by removing the rear panels and seat and installing the necessary lifting and towing equipment. The 'D'-sign on the roof indicates *Dépannage* (recovery). As customary in France, this commercial vehicle has its total weight (PT) and payload capacity (CU) painted on the body side.

36B

PRIVATE CAR CONVERSIONS

37A: This 1957 Belgian-operated American Plymouth sedan had a specially raised and strengthened rear suspension. The only other modifications included removal of the bootlid and the fitting of a fixed-position tubular steel hoisting frame.

37B: A French Ford dealer converted this Mk. 1 Ford 'Cortina'. After removing the rear body panels, it was equipped with a fixed chain-hoist.

37C: Another Anglo-French recovery vehicle was this highly unusual converted Jaguar Mk 2 of the 1960s, which, if nothing else, doubled up as an eye-catching visiting card for its owners. Fitted with a tubular boom structure with chain-hoist, it was undoubtedly one of the fastest wreckers in the world.

37A

37B

37C

38 : Even before World War I, in 1913, Merryweather & Sons Ltd., of Greenwich, London, world-famous fire appliance manufacturers, had supplied a unique recovery outfit to the Rio de Janeiro Fire Brigade. This was based on a chain-driven high-loading chassis, featuring a specially designed gantry hoist moveable throughout the entire body length on rails located outside the body.

39A : A close-up of the lifting mechanism as featured on the Merryweather machine shows that 'jib' elevation was rope-controlled and lifting accomplished with the aid of a Triplex block and chain hoist system.

39B : A 1917 Cadillac formed the basis for this Holmes Model 485 double-boom rig. This vehicle originally entered service with Baker's Garage as a general tow truck. Ernest Holmes equipment was not added until 1923.

39C : Not all Holmes recovery outfits were of the double-boom type. The Model 110, for example, was a fixed design bolted direct to the chassis and equipped for manual operation. This Ford Model TT has a c. 1920 Studebaker Tourer on suspended tow.

39D : This smartly turned out Austin 'Twenty', preserved by Mr. M. Quick, of Handcross, Sussex, was originally a taxicab when delivered new in 1926. Powered by a 4-cylinder petrol engine, it was converted into a light recovery outfit some years ago and is now a regular attender at old vehicle rallies throughout the British Isles.

39B

39D

39A

39C

40A

40B

40A: After smashing through a dry stone wall, a Karrier lorry was successfully recovered by an 'RAF'-Type Leyland equipped with 5 tons capacity Harvey Frost salvage crane, one of the first types produced by that Company. Damage to the Karrier was negligible!

40B: This Studebaker of c. 1927 vintage was equipped with a heavy-duty twin-boom recovery rig. Winching was manually-operated from the winding drums on either side of the wrecker supports. It was operated by the Studebaker importer in the Netherlands.

40C: Similarly, a number of Morris-Commercial dealers were also 'patriotic'. This D-Series 6-wheeler of 1928 was operated by the Company's Service & Repair Department at the main Soho (Birmingham) plant. It used a virtually standard wooden dropside body incorporating a light single-lift crane of 2/3 tons capacity. Note the overall tracks for the rear wheels stowed on the running board and the workbench (with vice) at the forward end of the body.

40C

41A: The 6 × 6 British FWD of 1929 was an unusual machine. Built by FWD Motors Ltd. at Slough, Bucks., production was later transferred to AEC's Southall works, incorporating many AEC components. It was supplied to the British military authorities both as an artillery tractor and as a recovery vehicle. The latter featured a manual winch at the forward end of the body, and all versions had planetary hub reduction gears.

41B: Examples of the R6T, as this FWD was known, eventually found their way into 'civvy street'. This version received a new 'cab' and specially fabricated recovery crane. For some years it operated in the Leeds area of Yorkshire.

41C: Delivered to the Indian Army in 1930, this was a rare version of the Morris-Commercial D-Series 6-wheeler. It had a twin-lift crane, open cab, radiator guard and additional front towing equipment.

41A

41B

41C

43A

43B

42 : The London Passenger Transport Board's Karrier recovery outfit of the 1930's was packed with an incredible array of recovery equipment for use in connection with tram and trolleybus services. The crane itself was of the full-slew type, manually-controlled, and with chain lifting equipment. On the crane deck were a multitude of recovery aids, including ratchet jacks, ballast weights and blocks, baulks of timber, oxy-acetylene cutting equipment, etc. The cab was extended at the rear to incorporate a crew and workshop area and above this was an extensible inspection platform for dealing with fouled overhead wires.

43A : The Weaver Mfg. Co., of Springfield, Ohio, designed and built an extensive range of garage and recovery equipment which was also available in many other parts of the world. Harvey Frost of Bishop's Stortford imported Weaver products for the UK market. Typical was the Type G Auto Crane with manual operation and chain hoist system. The chassis in this instance was a 30-cwt Ford AA of 1930/1.

43D

43C

43B : This Bedford 2-tonner is claimed to have been the first recovery vehicle based on a Bedford chassis. Delivered to Messrs Vincent Greenhous, of Wrexham, North Wales, in 1934, it later passed to Hughes' Garage, Chirk, Denbighs., with whom it spent the major part of its working life. It was subsequently sold to W. J. Harmer & Sons, bus proprietors, of Southsea, near Wrexham.

43C : A popular practice at one time was the conversion of existing box-bodied vehicles for use as recovery outfits. This 30-cwt Commer N2 of 1938 vintage was converted thus soon after World War II. The work was carried out by the operators, Messrs Grimaldi Bros., of St. Albans, Herts, who cut away the rear portion of the body, equipping this with a manual chain hoist and 'towing ambulance'. Note the winch handle point on the body side.

43D : Ford of America's first 'cab-over-engine' trucks were announced in late 1938. This Ernest Holmes wrecker, a manually-operated twin-boom Model 515, was mounted on one of these chassis, a 134-in wheelbase Model 99W powered by a V-8 petrol engine.

WORLD WAR II AND ITS EFFECTS

44A

44B

44C

One might wonder how the wrecker and recovery vehicle fields would have developed had there been no World War II. Not only did this conflict result in new vehicle recovery techniques but also in the use of heavy-duty all-wheel drive machines, which remain in plentiful supply right up to the present day.

New names entered the design and manufacturing side of the business and older ones became well established. Gar Wood Industries Inc., Sasgen Derrick Co. and The Silent Hoist Co. were three American concerns which, by 1945, were famous in this field. All have now ceased production under these names.

44D

44A : First of the single-boom outfits employed by the American armed forces in World War II was the M1, based on Kenworth or Ward LaFrance 6 × 6 chassis, powered by 145-bhp Continental engines driving through 10-speed transmissions. There were several variants. This Series 4 Ward LaFrance, with some post-war alterations, was distinguishable from its predecessors by having a curved boom.

44B : The M1A1 models, successors to the M1, first appeared in 1943. Both versions, again by Kenworth and Ward LaFrance, were now identical. Standard equipment included a 5 tons capacity slewing boom by Gar Wood and power winches fore and aft.

44C : Photographed in the Netherlands in 1965, a much modified Series 5 Model 1000 Ward LaFrance M1A1 illustrates what can be done to make a basically austere military vehicle into an attractive but functional machine.

44D : The US Army Air Force had its own type of wrecker, based on a special version of the standard 7½-ton 6 × 6 chassis of the period. The Biederman shown here was known as the Type C-2. A unique feature of this type of machine was the semi-trailer coupling for operation with flat semi-trailers for the conveyance of wrecked aircraft. The wrecking boom was supplied by the Silent Hoist Co., of Brooklyn, New York.

WORLD WAR II AND ITS EFFECTS

45A-B: The Mack LM-SW, a tandem-drive 6-wheeler supplied to the British and Canadian armed forces under the Lend-Lease scheme, was built as a single- or double-boom outfit. The single-boom version was supplied to Britain with Gar Wood body and equipment. Billy Smart's Circus owned one of these for a number of years after the war but body and equipment were later transferred to a 6-ton 6 × 6 NM-Series Mack, illustrated here.

45C: Another Mack truck of World War II origin which was very suitable for a heavy recovery vehicle was the 7½-ton 6 × 6 NO-Series. Like the other contemporary Mack six-wheelers (with the exception of the NR-Series) it had a large-capacity six-cylinder petrol engine. The NO was unusual in having a near-vertical steering column, situated at the extreme left-hand side of its full-width cab and a step-down type front axle in which the front-wheel drive was entirely by means of helical gears and without the customary constant-velocity joints. During the 1960s the British Army released a fair number of well-maintained NO's—also known as 'Super Macks'—and many if not most of these were subsequently fitted with heavy and straightforward recovery gear, exemplified by this 'King of the Road' with modified cab but near-original GS body.

45A

45B

45C

46A: Wm. C. Jackson, Managing Director of Dial-Holmes (England) Ltd., was formerly General Manager of the Chaseside Motor Co., Enfield, Middx., where he designed an unusual rear hoist system for installation on an ex-military Diamond T 980 tractor, previously used for tank recovery and transportation. The lifting system, which used the vehicle's original power winching capabilities, is seen to advantage in this simulated traffic accident.

46B: Minor differences between the 980 and 981 Diamond T include a 300-ft winch cable and two winch cable roller sheaves at the rear of the 980, with a 500-ft cable, three cable sheaves at rear and a roller assembly in the front bumper of the 981. This example of the latter was acquired in 1970 from Messrs Robert Wynn & Sons Ltd., heavy hauliers, and fitted with an 8 tons capacity Harvey Frost twin-lift salvage crane.

46C: The 4-ton 969 Series Diamond T 6 × 6 saw many uses. Introduced in 1941, one such application was as a double-boom power wrecker using Ernest Holmes equipment. This modified version had a custom-built cab, lengthened bonnet to accommodate a larger engine and a revised front winch system.

46D: A rare version of the 969 was used by the US Chemical Warfare Service to lift and transport heavy chemical containers. One such was employed by W. W. Drinkwater Ltd., contractors, of North London. Although the crane body was not original, the unusual frame over the cab was standard on these outfits.

46A

46B

46C

46D

47A

47B

47C

47D

47A: During World War II, the normal-control version of the FWD SU-Series 4 × 4 truck found popularity as an airfield snow-fighter. Examples were also equipped with Holmes W.45 power wrecking gear for 'light' aircraft handling with the Royal Canadian Air Force. To provide maximum reach, the double-boom equipment was mounted over the rear axle.
47B: A number of lighter truck chassis were kitted out as bomb service trucks. These were used for loading, unloading and hauling bomb-carrying trailers. An identifying feature was the unusual lifting gantry carried by these machines, exemplified by this Chevrolet-based model powered by a 93-bhp 6-cylinder engine. Dual rear tyres and cab were post-war modifications.
47C: When it was found that GMC could not cope with the demand for 6 × 6 trucks in the 2½-ton class, similar models were introduced by other manufacturers. Studebaker's equivalent was the US6, powered by an 87-bhp Hercules engine. This short-wheelbase unit was later fitted with a crane and saw many years of peacetime service in Belgium.
47D: Among the first production military 6-ton 6 × 6 trucks produced in any quantity during World War II were virtually identical models by White and Corbitt (the 666 and 50SD6 respectively). The front end of this example was modified somewhat and the fixed recovery crane used the vehicle's original power winch and cable.

48A: Brockway's B666 was also in the 6-ton 6 × 6 class but was of longer wheelbase for use as a bridge erection truck. The example shown has a coachbuilt cab and Dial-Holmes twin-boom equipment. 10 tons capacity winches were fitted at front and rear.

48B: Between 1942 and 1945 the Pacific Car & Foundry Co., of Seattle, Washington, supplied armoured and 'soft skin' 6 × 6 tractors for tank recovery work. Robert Wynn & Sons Ltd., of Newport, Mon., later converted six of the armoured variety (known as the M26) for heavy haulage applications. One was equipped with a special rear crane jib for use both as a general lifting crane and as a recovery unit. Note the reinforced wheels.

48C: What must surely have been one of the largest recovery vehicles anywhere was also based on a Pacific 6 × 6. This, however, was the 'soft skin' version (M26A1). Based near the motorway at Amersfoort, Netherlands, the monster featured a heavy-duty extensible rear jib operated from the original power winch located behind the cab. The cable was run beneath the cab, over the frame at the front of the vehicle and thence to the crane boom.

48B

48A

48C

WORLD WAR II AND ITS EFFECTS

49A : The White M3A1 was a scout car powered by a 110-bhp 6-cylinder Hercules engine. This example, owned by a French repair shop, was only slightly modified. Lifting equipment consisted of a single chain hoist on a fixed jib.

49B : At one time, a British garage and repair business employed a converted Canadian GM armoured truck, Model C15TA, for light and medium recovery work. Garage modifications included a revised windscreen layout, minor body alterations and ballast weights at the front.

49A

49D

49B

49C

49E

49C : For many years a Ruislip, Middx., garage ran this neatly proportioned 8-cwt Canadian Ford F8, formerly a wireless truck. The simple manually-operated lifting crane was ideal for light car recovery.

49D/E : The 1942–45 American Dodge ¾-ton 4 × 4 T214 Series has always been particularly popular with garage proprietors in France, as well as in other countries. Especially low-mileage 'command cars' with winch fetched high prices at Government auctions and the two examples shown were turned into wreckers during the late seventies when such vehicles were still being demobbed by the French Army. Both have been provided with closed cabs assembled from the remains of old passenger cars but the lifting gear is quite different.

50A: F. I. Bates & Son Ltd. completely re-bodied a Canadian F60H Ford 6 × 4 3-tonner, equipping it with a fixed-position Harvey Frost twin-lift salvage crane. Final drive arrangement was rather unusual, only the leading rear axle and steering axle being powered. The third axle was a trailing unit.

50B: The 15-cwt MW-Series Bedford was one of the most common British-built 15-cwt trucks used by the Allies in World War II. Photographed in France, the example shown featured an overhead gantry system with chain hoist equipment.

50C: Largest production British 3-ton 4 × 4 in World War II was the 72-bhp Bedford QL which, naturally enough, found countless civilian users after the war. The lifting equipment shown here was designed and built by Mr. Peter Hoblyn, proprietor of Recovery Units, Lower Kingswood, Surrey, in 1970. With a lift capacity of approximately 6 tons, an ex-WD Thompson 2-speed manual winch was used for light duties whilst a Gar Wood power winch coped with heavier work.

50D: A truly remarkable machine was this weird 6 × 6 four-wheel steer outfit owned by Messrs Michell Motors Ltd., of Chicklade, Wilts. This was based on a QL chassis with added second steering axle. Power was supplied by a Perkins R6 engine, driving through a Bedford main transmission and Bedford QL and Chevrolet transfer boxes. Winch equipment consisted of a Turner power winch and Scammell manual unit. Snowplough attachments were mounted at the front.

50C

50A

50B

50D

51A

51B

51C

51A: An example of the Albion FT15N, a low-silhouette 6 × 6 field artillery tractor introduced in small quantities towards the end of the war, received a complete ex-Services Holmes double-boom wrecking unit and body, resulting in a neatly proportioned wrecker of ample capacity.

51B: The first full-scale use of the overhead gantry system came about at the beginning of World War II, when Crossley, Guy, Dodge (USA), Leyland and Canadian Ford 6-wheeled chassis were adapted for this purpose. Shown is the Guy FBAX. When travelling, the gantry was moved forward over the cab and when operating, if a higher lift was called for, the gantry's forward end could be lowered to the body floor and locked in position.

51C: Austin's tandem-drive K6 superseded the forward-control types in 1944 and many later found their way to civilian operators. Retaining its original body, this specimen was used for carrying earthmover tyres.

51D: The British Airports Authority converted an Austin K6 for use as a recovery unit in the then new London Airport (Heathrow) Tunnel. If necessary, it could assist the recovery of wrecked aircraft. This machine had a Harvey Frost twin-lift crane, with a smart streamlined body by Spurlings Motor Bodies Ltd.

51D

52A : Scammell Lorries' 30 tons capacity tank transporter tractor, type TRMU/30, based on the 'Pioneer' 6-wheeled chassis, also found considerable popularity as a recovery vehicle. Power was supplied by a Gardner 6LW diesel and a Scammell 8-ton vertical winch was standard equipment.

52B : Scammells also built two types of heavy breakdowns. Most common was the SV/2S, with Herbert Morris hand-actuated sliding jib. This had three positions—long lift (2 tons), short lift (3 tons) and travelling. Overall chains could be used for the rear wheels, as shown here.

52C : The 'Pioneer' was a common choice of civilian operators. Many have gone so far as to fit completely new bodies as seen here. Cab,

crew and workshop area were integral, with through access to the fabricated crane at the rear. This crane worked off the vehicle's original winch system. Note, also, the 'boxed-in' front wings.

52D : Of all British ex-Services trucks engaged in recovery work, the AEC 'Matador' 4 × 4 model was perhaps the most common. One of the first to operate these was the London Passenger Transport Board, whose 'Matadors' were equipped with weatherproof workshop areas and 8-ton Harvey Frost slewing cranes. These were in service for many years and the Board's crews were renowned for the speed with which they could right an overturned double-decker bus using one of these AEC's.

52B

52C

52A

52D

WORLD WAR II AND ITS EFFECTS

53A : Many 'Matadors', like some of the Scammells, were rebodied for civilian use. Messrs Stewart & Ardern, BLMC dealers and coachbuilders, designed and built their own fully-integral body for a 'Matador' equipped with Harvey Frost 8 tons capacity crane. Note the twin roof warning lamps and kerb sighting window.

53B : This 'Matador' carried a Dodge D-Series cab, modified to clear the standard front towing jaw. Lifting equipment, assembled in the operator's own workshops, comprised a single-lift boom with cable run off the original winch drum.

53C : Equipped with an 8-ton Harvey Frost crane, this 6 × 6 AEC 0854, based on similar lines to the smaller 'Matador' 4 × 4 design, had a neatly styled integral body featuring 'straight-through' access from cab to workshop area and specially designed rear towing equipment.

53A

53B

53C

DAY AND NIGHT
BREAKDOWN & RECOVERY SERVICE

538 CL

54: In 1944 and 1945 AEC produced 151 armoured command vehicles based on a normal-control version of their 6 × 6 chassis, known as the 0856. These had the more powerful 150-bhp engine driving through an 8-speed transmission. A few were later purchased by Messrs Mann Egerton & Co. Ltd., the bodies removed and new cabs, bodywork and hydraulic salvage equipment fitted. One was placed in service by Mann Egerton themselves, equipped with a 10-ton lifting boom, rear power winch and oxy-acetylene cutting equipment.

55A: This neat little job was a former Italian Army Fiat/Spa CL39 4 × 4 1-tonner. The crane jib was elevated by hand, bolts being inserted through the support members as the jib was lifted. Power was supplied by a 25-bhp Spa engine driving through a 5-speed transmission.

55B: Some examples of Faun's ZR heavy wheeled tractors were adapted to run on rails, using specially flanged wheels. This model was referred to as the ZRS. An example of the standard road-going version was maintained by the Baden Fire Service as a recovery outfit, with twin-boom equipment located over the rear axle where the ballast box was previously mounted. Storage space for breakdown tools and equipment was minimal, the original crewcab being retained—baulks of timber were carried on the running boards and winch cable across the front bumper.

55C: Half-track vehicles were well-favoured by the German military authorities. The Krauss-Maffei Sd.Kfz.7, an 8-ton medium semi-track machine, was powered by a 140-bhp Maybach engine. The Austrian Fire Service should be more than proud of this beautifully turned out version equipped with a power-operated double-boom wrecking outfit.

55D: The Swedish Volvo TVC 6 × 6, introduced as an artillery tractor back in 1942, was powered by a 135-bhp 6-cylinder petrol engine. It had independent coil spring suspension with swing axles and twin propeller shafts to the front wheels. The single tubular boom shown here could be swung to left or right and raised or lowered. Winch cables could be run through sheaves at front or rear of the vehicle.

55A

55B

55C

55D

THE AEC 'MILITANT'

In 1952 AEC Ltd., of Southall, Middx., developed the 'Militant I', a powerful six-wheel drive chassis, designed for military and other cross-country applications. In British military circles it succeeded the 6 × 6 version of the wartime 'Matador' 4 × 4 and a number of Mk.I's were still in service in 1970.

However, 1966 saw the introduction of the 'Militant III', an impressive giant powered by a 226-bhp 12.47-litre diesel driving through a 12-speed transmission, of which the majority in British military service have been equipped as medium recovery outfits. This has now replaced many of the famous Scammell 'Explorer' 6 × 6 recovery models.

56A

56B

56A: This impressive 'Militant I' was one of a few supplied to Ghana in 1963, each fitted with a 10 tons capacity Mann Egerton power-driven turntable crane.

56B: All Wheel Drive Ltd. adapted a small quantity of 'Militant I' chassis for carrying Blaw-Knox excavators. Criton Engineering Ltd., of Orsett, Essex, later converted one of these for recovery work, retaining the original outriggers and turntable base and adding a T.20 TFL hydraulic crane. All coachbuilding was undertaken in the Company's own works, using Atkinson wrap-round screens for the cab front. Performance included a drawbar capacity of 20,000 lb and in service the machine has successfully started a 40 tons gross train weight on a 1 in 6 gradient. Total cost of conversion was about £7,000!

THE AEC 'MILITANT'

57A-B: Introduced in 1966, the 'Militant III' has been supplied in greater numbers as a medium recovery outfit than in any other form. Designed as a recovery rig by Scammell Lorries Ltd., Watford, it features a 240° slewing hydraulic-powered single-boom crane supplied by Coles Cranes Ltd. and all other recovery equipment by Transport Equipment (Thornycroft) Ltd. Maximum speed is nearly 50 mph.
57C: A close-up of the rear of the machine shows the single-piece land anchor (lower foreground), winch cable and spring pulley (centre), and the triangular spacer bar (top centre) for use when coping with a suspended tow. With the land anchor in use, a maximum winch pull of up to 30 tons is possible.

57A

57B

57C

THE SCAMMELL 'EXPLORER'

Scammell's 6 × 6 'Explorer' replaced the wartime 'Pioneer' recovery unit as the standard breakdown vehicle used by the British forces during the early Fifties. Recovery equipment was similar to the earlier model but the machine's overall height was noticeably greater and power was supplied by a Meadows petrol engine as standard, specially adapted by Scammell Lorries Ltd., for use in the 'Explorer'. There were few jobs it could not tackle with its 15 tons capacity winch and 3-ton maximum lift crane.

59A

58 : This view of one of the first 'Explorer' recovery vehicles shows the hoist mechanism and rear bogie articulation qualities. Recovery equipment was similar to that of the 'Pioneer' version (Figs. 52B and 52C). The military designation of this 'Explorer' was FV11301.
59A : In 1959 a special petrol-engined version of more modern appearance was produced for the Egyptian Government. This followed an identical batch (except for right-hand drive and diesel engines) sold to the New Zealand Government in 1956. Note the overall chains over the rear bogie wheels.
59B : Many of the original 'Explorer' models are now with civilian operators. Messrs Caffyns Ltd., for instance, a leading garage chain in the South of England, have re-equipped part of their 'Pioneer' fleet with 'Explorers'.
59C : Another example, operated in Kent, has been beautifully adapted for civilian use and is seen here with the jib in the maximum extended position. Note the heavy chains ready for use and the distinctive safety markings on the rear mudflaps.

59B

59C

THE US 'M-SERIES' 6 × 6

The earliest 'M-Series' models were built by Reo in 1950/51 and popularly known as 'Eager Beavers'. They succeeded the wartime GMC 2½-ton 6 × 6, the basic and most common versions being the M34 and M35 with cargo bodies.

The basic concept, of course, was US Army Ordnance 'property', resulting in other manufacturers also receiving contracts for their production. These included Studebaker and, following the acquisition of the Studebaker truck plant by Kaiser Jeep Corporation, by the latter and, later, American Motors.

There have been dozens of variants of the 'M-Series', amongst which were the M60 and M108 wreckers. Many have now been withdrawn and are undertaking valuable work in the civilian recovery field.

In the heavier (5-ton) range of 'M-Series' 6 × 6 trucks there were five wrecker versions (M62, M246, M543, M816 and M819) but their use by civilians is less frequent. Wrecking equipment was mainly by Austin-Western and Gar Wood and of the hydraulic type, although Gar Wood also produced a World War II-pattern mechanical slewing jib variant.

60A

60A: The M60, designed and built as a wrecker for military use, incorporated a hydraulic-powered slewing boom, with powered extension and luffing. A single-lift system was employed. Equipment was by Austin-Western.
60B: Automobielbedrijf R. A. Mimiasie NV, of Rotterdam, Netherlands, are specialists in the preparation and conversion of the 'M-Series' for civilian applications. In many instances, the original power unit has been replaced by a new engine—in this case a DAF—and the vehicle reassembled after being stripped to the last nut and bolt.

60B

61A

61C

61B

61A: Another Mimiasie conversion, again with a new DAF engine, carried a new coachbuilt cab but was otherwise near to original specification. Note the heavy front winch.

61B: This recovery vehicle was based on a standard 'M-Series' 2½-ton 6 × 6 chassis and featured a front winch as a non-original addition. It had a manually-actuated twin-lift salvage crane and two floodlights. In the British Isles this was a rather unusual wrecker.

61C: In recent years the Dutch firm of R. A. Mimiasie has marketed completely reworked 'M-Series' trucks under the tradename RAM. This is a 5-ton 6 × 6 Model M543 with its original US Army Gar Wood hydraulic telescopic crane (M62 was similar but with Austin-Western crane with single lift cylinder). The MAN front end, cab and diesel engine are part of the RAM conversion.

OTHER POST-WORLD WAR II TYPES

62A

Although a greater percentage of wreckers and recovery vehicles employed after the war were based on plentiful supplies of ex-Services chassis, it is true to say that many brand-new chassis were also used, principally by franchise holders of a particular marque (e.g. Commer, Dodge, Ford, Bedford, etc).

As time progressed, more modern ex-Services equipment was purchased and by 1970 many recovery operators were boasting collections of new ex-Services outfits displaying an almost minimal mileage 'on the clock'; such has been the turnover of military transport and equipment in recent years that some of the luckier buyers have managed to obtain machines with only 'factory mileage'. In addition to

62B

62C

62D

62A : This American Ford pick-up of immediate post-war years continues to operate regularly in France, despite an apparently bent chassis! A tubular steel fabricated hoist is mounted at the rear.

62B : Mill Garage, Norwich, designs and builds its own recovery equipment. Among the more unusual types was a 6-wheeled conversion of the Series I Land-Rover. The chassis frame was extended at the rear and a trailing axle fitted. This provided greater stability, particularly when towing. Lifting equipment, using a battery-powered winch, was most unusual for this class of vehicle.

62C : Extremely rare in the United Kingdom, this 4 × 4 Oshkosh W-703D is believed to have been operated originally by the USAF. Powered by a Hercules diesel engine, this model was introduced towards the end of 1949. Wrecking equipment was by Dial-Holmes (England) Ltd.

62D : The Douglas 'Transporter' 4 × 4 timber tractor used AEC 'Matador' running gear and associated components but had a shorter wheelbase. Richard Read, of Longhope, Glos., adapted one of these for use as a recovery outfit, here seen winching an ERF 8-wheeler out of a roadside ditch.

being cheaper than new vehicles, these machines also fulfil the multifarious requirements of the recovery specialist, being of rugged construction and equipped with all-wheel drive, power winches, powerful engines and other advantages.

Since 1970 there has been increasing interest in the use of heavy multi-wheeled goods vehicles and new commercial models as a basis for recovery work. On the multi-wheeled front, the short-wheelbase 8-wheeler is a popular choice, particularly with general haulage operators of such machines. 6-wheeled models can also be found and new 4-wheeled commercials (e.g. Fig. 3C) are readily adapted for medium-duty recovery work up to 16 tons gross.

63A

63B

63C

63A: Equipment carriers and emergency tenders in the German Fire Service are frequently based on Mercedes-Benz chassis. This L315 7-tonner, bodied by Metz and delivered in 1953, had a 10 tons capacity hydraulic crane by Demag and front-mounted power winch, both indispensable for vehicle recovery and general salvage work.

63B: The Humber FV1600 Series 1-ton 4 × 4, powered by a 120-bhp Rolls-Royce B.60 Mk.5A 6-cylinder petrol engine, is no longer in use with the British armed forces. The cargo version (shown) was referred to as the FV1601. L. W. Vass Ltd., dealers in ex-Services vehicles

and equipment, offered this recovery truck conversion as standard, equipped with a 3 tons capacity Harvey Frost salvage crane.

63C: With a 3-ton payload, the French military Simca-Unic F594 WML 4 × 4 was designed for on- and off-highway travel, and offered on the civilian market as the 'Cargo'. In this instance, the original canvas roof has been replaced and the ribbed metal doors were removed. The all-steel body was original but crane equipment, operating off the vehicle's power winch, was not. This model was introduced in 1956.

64A: Another French machine, the Latil M16TRPZ, was capable of lifting light tanks as well as normal road-going machines. Tanks could only be lifted when the special stabilizing poles (seen here in the stowed position) were used.

64B: A magnificent example of a heavy wrecker could be found in the Willème CG 8 × 4 hydraulic aircraft recovery vehicle, designed for operation at 80 tons gross. This was also a French design, introduced at the Paris Motor Show in 1956, and equipped with an Applevage 18 tons capacity all-hydraulic recovery crane. Power came from a 220-bhp 13·5-litre 6-cylinder petrol engine. Because of legal width restrictions on the road, the rear bogie outer wheels were quickly detachable.

64C: Rootes Group dealers of the Fifties operated both forward- and normal-control Commer recovery vehicles. The former was the underfloor-engined machine which made its debut in 1948. Within a fortnight of entering service, this 5-ton Harvey Frost design was busy retrieving a car from the bottom of an embankment.

64D: In 1958 Rootes of Maidstone supplied a unique 4 × 4 version of the underfloor-engined Commer to the main Rootes Group dealers in Manchester. It is believed that the chassis was first designed as a military prototype. It had an integral body containing a hand winch and an 8 tons capacity Harvey Frost slewing crane at the rear.

64A

64C

64B

64D

OTHER POST-WORLD WAR II TYPES

65A: A 6 × 4 Foden FG6/20, powered by a 112-bhp Gardner 6LW engine, was delivered in 1961, for use in Kuwait. Fitted with an 8 tons capacity slewing Harvey Frost salvage crane, a special feature was the 80,000 lb line pull Darlington capstan winch mounted behind the cab.

65B: One of the more unusual 8-wheeled models operating in the United Kingdom in 1969 was this Thornycroft 'Trusty' with AEC grille. The chassis frame had been terminated immediately to the rear of the driving axles and a hydraulically elevated single-piece steel girder boom was mounted on the chassis. Fixed chains at the end of this boom were used to secure the damaged vehicle.

65C: Carmans of Northampton also had a Foden FG6/20, equipped with an 8 tons capacity Harvey Frost crane. This, however, was mounted lower than in the previous example and could even deal with a fully-laden 22 tons gross 6-wheeler.

65A

65B

65C

66A

66B

66C

66A: A little known British manufacturer of recovery cranes and associated equipment is the Vehicle & Plant Supply Co., of West Drayton, Middx. Recovery equipment, and many other types of steel truck bodywork, are built only to special order under the VAPSCO trade name. H. Sabey & Co. Ltd., a regular customer, had this short-wheelbase Albion 'Chieftain' converted from a tipper into a compact all-hydraulic recovery outfit. This had a fixed hook at the rear and carried a power winch. Note the winch guide roller beneath the body side.

66B: The Gloucestershire Fire Service have two particularly interesting recovery and salvage outfits. One, a 4 × 4 R-Series Bedford, was equipped by Messrs Reynolds Boughton. The low body incorporated a number of special equipment lockers with roller shutters and a unique Yale fork-lift attachment at the rear. This carried a tubular steel hoist which could be raised and lowered in the same way that the original forks would have been. At the front of the vehicle a Boughton power winch and land anchor provided winching facilities and additional weight to counterbalance the rear hoist.

66C: What had been intended purely as a promotional exercise by a North American operator resulted in a compact breakdown machine for the lightest applications. Basis of the special conversion was a wrecked Austin Mini, which was rebuilt and fitted with a manual hoist. All the characteristics of the biggest wreckers were included, such as roof marker lights, rotating amber warning light and air horns.

66D: The Austin 'Gipsy' 4 × 4 was not as successful as the Land-Rover. Largest users of the 'Gipsy' were BMC dealers, such as Caffyns Ltd., who used them for private car recovery work. A light and easily removable Harvey Frost crane is seen here.

66D

67A

67C

67B

67D

67A: The Berliet TBU.15 CLD was a 6 × 6 medium recovery vehicle equipped with a 10 tons capacity hydraulic slewing crane and two winches, one of which was located inside the cab. Most went to the French and Belgian armed forces but in 1965 two were supplied to the British forces in Germany through Alvis Ltd., of Coventry. These were the only two examples to carry the Alvis badge and one is seen here following an ex-Services auction sale at Ruddington, Notts.

67B: Shortly before the Dartford Tunnel was opened beneath the River Thames in 1963, the Tunnel Joint Committee took delivery of a fleet of recovery vehicles specially designed for ease of operation within the tunnel confines. For dealing with cars and medium-sized commercials up to 7 tons in weight, two Scammell 'Scarab' 3-wheeled 'mechanical horses' were each specially adapted by fitting dual rear wheels, 3 tons capacity Harvey Frost crane and front-mounted 'towing ambulance'.

67C: Another unusual machine operated by Mill Garage, of Norwich (Fig. 62B), was based on a Bedford TK-Series tractor unit. The fork-lift principle, as in the case of the Gloucestershire Fire Service R-Series Bedford (Fig. 66B), was applied here. In this instance, however, the winch cable could be run over the top of the fork-lift column to provide both improved stability when winching and increased winching height.

67D: Wrecker operators have to tackle a multitude of varying tasks— even earthmoving equipment can break down. This double-boom Holmes outfit based on a beautifully turned out tandem-drive Autocar handles a Trojan wheeled tractor shovel with ease.

OTHER POST-WORLD WAR II TYPES

68 : Based on an AEC 'Marshal' tiltcab chassis, and designed by Gloucestershire Fire Service personnel, this double-boom wrecker tackling a fog pile-up copes with anything from floods to railway disasters. The double-boom outfit is a Holmes 750 tested to a capacity of $23\frac{1}{2}$ tons on suspended tow and a straight lift of almost 14 tons. The forward compartments contain an inflatable rubber dinghy, outboard motor, portable electric generator, numerous electric tools and floodlamps, submersible pump, etc. for emergency and salvage work.

69A : The revolutionary 'Trailbak', developed by B. Dixon-Bate Ltd., of Chester, is designed to haulage contractors and other fleet owners in mind. Not only is it cheap and economical but it can also be fitted to any fifth wheel or automatic-coupling tractor unit. In this way, an operator does not have to maintain a complete recovery outfit; the 'Trailbak' can be secured to an existing tractor unit by two men in a matter of minutes and has a safe working load of $4\frac{1}{2}$ tons.

69B : An L406 Mercedes-Benz is the ideal basis for passenger car recovery work. This example has a tubular steel hoisting beam, with cable run off a battery-powered winch. Towbars and other essentials are securely fastened to the body.

69C : Of a similar capacity, the Fiat 616 equipped for recovery work by Orecchia & C. SpA, features an extensible hydraulic lifting boom with single hook, again battery-controlled. Control levers are visible at the rear of the vehicle.

69D : The German Fire Service, and other authorities, purchase their recovery outfits new. Practically all feature hydraulic actuation, extensive jibs and drag winches. They are designed to tackle successfully all tasks that may be set before them. Shown is a Mercedes-Benz 4 × 4-based unit.

69B

69C

69A

69D

70A: In some areas, a 6 × 6 Mercedes-Benz, such as this LAK 2624, is even more useful. Operated by the Saltzburg Brigade, this example has a Krupp-Ardelt hydraulic crane similar to those incorporated in that Company's truck-crane range. As can be seen, it is still most useful as a recovery crane and has ample reach to be of special use in larger pile-ups.

70B: French equivalent is the Saviem 6 × 6 Model EPG 226W. Power is supplied by a MAN 6-cylinder diesel. The full-slewing hydraulic crane, which is extensible, can deal with a gross load of some 15 tons and is provided with stabilizers and rear roller-type land anchors. A winch is mounted at the rear.

70C: The only Scammell 'Himalayan' wrecker in the British Isles was recently completed by the Norwich-based Mill Garage. Employing a chassis originally ordered for export to India, the Company expanded the one-man cab into a full-width type and assembled the slewing hydraulic crane themselves. Capable of lifting 22 tons gross and of extending to 36 ft in height, it has been designed with the recovery of overturned container vehicles in mind.

70A

70B

70C

OTHER POST-WORLD WAR II TYPES

71A: A most unusual machine, using a Scania L80 S42 normal-control chassis/cab with 10-speed transmission, has been developed in Sweden. Designed for use as a fire service emergency appliance, its most unique feature is a Model 5501 HIAB hydraulic loading crane at the rear, ideal for vehicle recovery and other lifting duties up to a maximum of 5·8 tons. At the front, the chassis frame has been extended to take a power winch, designed and built by Östbergs Fabriks AB, Alfta, adequately protected by a second brushguard. Coachwork is by the Vellinge Coachbuilding Co., with fire-fighting apparatus by Henrikssons Brandredskap, Stockholm.

71B-C: The Swiss bulk liquid haulage concern, Transag (Transporte AG), uses a particularly interesting double-boom wrecker. If one of their tankers is involved in an accident it is more than likely that a liquid, sometimes volatile, is also involved. Before moving, say, an overturned tanker it is necessary to pump the tank dry. Thus, a wrecker and a second tanker are required. The new recovery outfit incorporates the best of both worlds; behind the cab is a 5000-litre tank and at the rear a Holmes 600 twin-boom power wrecker. The whole is mounted on a Mercedes-Benz chassis with single-tyred trailing axle conversion.

71B

71A

71C

INDEX

ACKNOWLEDGEMENTS

This volume was compiled largely from historic source material in the library of the Olyslager Organisation, plus many photographs and other material kindly provided or loaned by the following:
Dial-Holmes (England) Ltd., Tracel Fabrications Ltd., Weld/Built Body Co., Bendix Westinghouse Ltd., Ailsa Trucks Ltd., Harvey Frost & Co. Ltd., Mann Egerton & Co. Ltd., London Fire Brigade, Reynolds Boughton Ltd., London Transport Executive, Mill Garage, the Commercial Vehicle & Road Transport Club, DNM Automotive, and the private collections of Alfred Krenn, Peter Davies and Bart H. Vanderveen.
Thanks are also extended to David J. Voller and the many other organisations and individuals without whose assistance this volume would not have been possible.